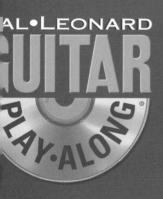

HAL•LEONARD
GUITAR
PLAY•ALONG

ACOUSTIC METAL

M000121931

CONTENTS

Tracking, mixing, and mastering by Jake Johnson
All guitars by Doug Boduch
Bass by Tom McGirr
Keyboards by Warren Wiegratz
Drums by Scott Schroedl

ISBN 0-634-08401-1

Visit Hal Leonard Online at www.halleonard.com

HAL•LEONARD®
CORPORATION
7777 W. BLUEMOUND RD. P.O. BOX 13819
MILWAUKEE, WISCONSIN 53213

Every Rose Has Its Thorn

Words and Music by Bobby Dall, Brett Michaels, Bruce Johannesson and Rikki Rocket

Tune down 1/2 step:
(low to high) Eb-Ab-Db-Gb-Bb-Eb

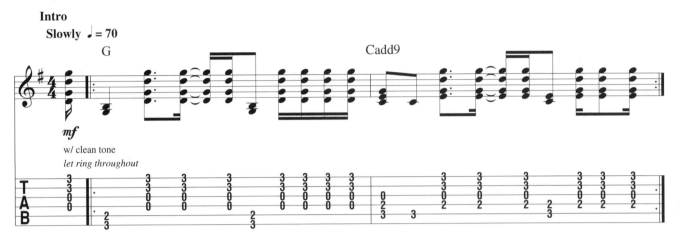

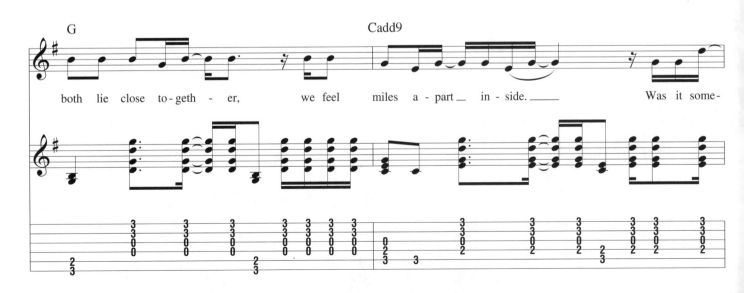

4

5

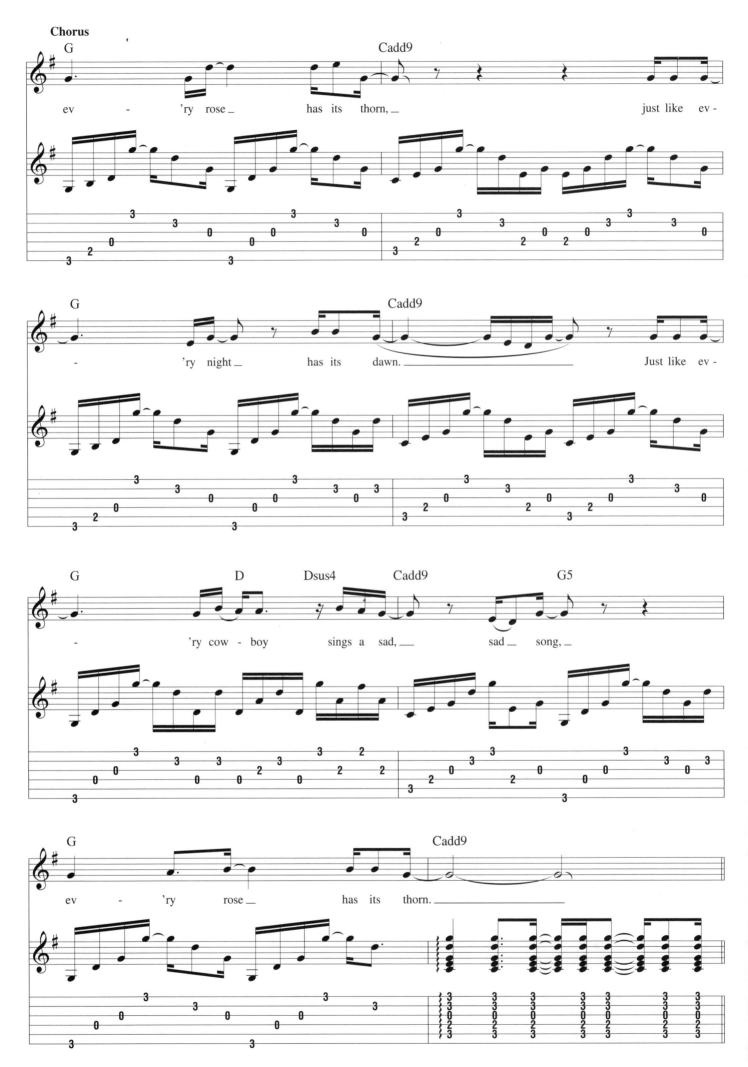

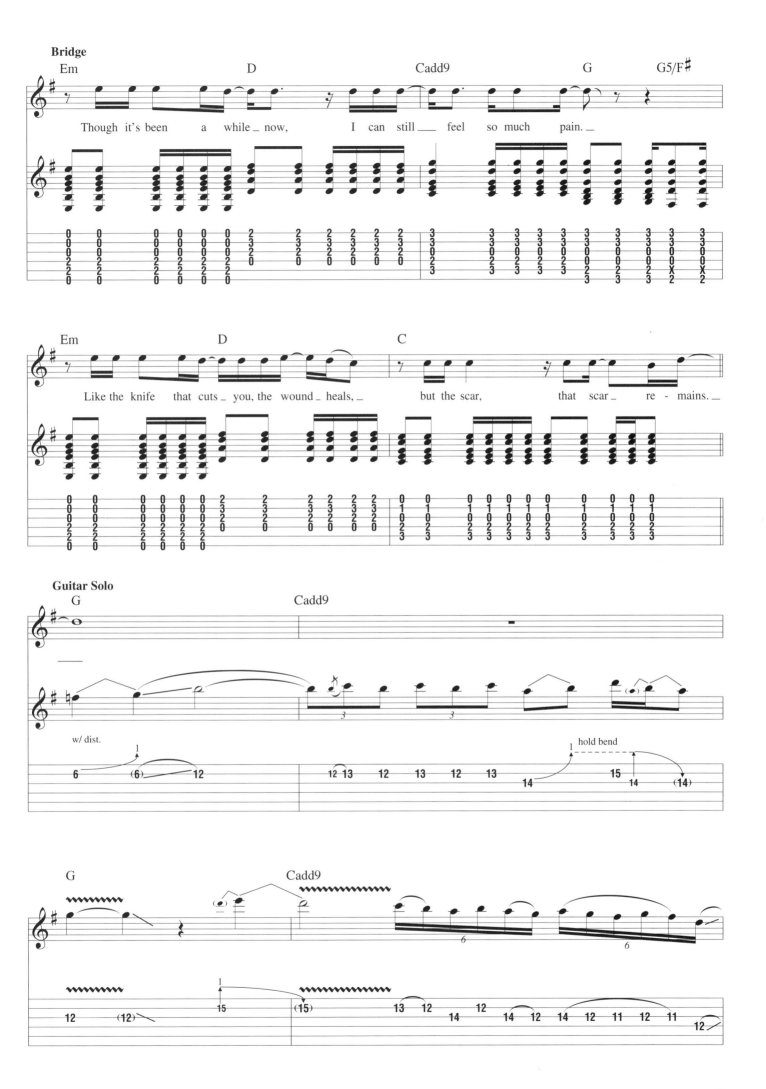

Bridge

Though it's been a while _ now, I can still _ feel so much pain. _

Like the knife that cuts _ you, the wound _ heals, _ but the scar, that scar _ re - mains. _

Guitar Solo

w/ dist.

hold bend

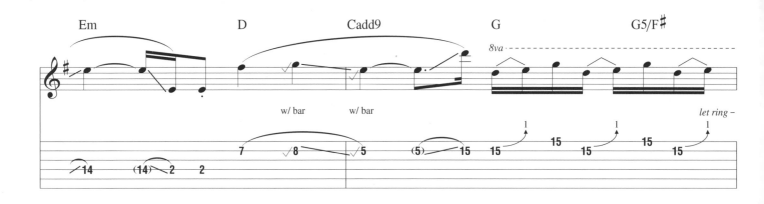

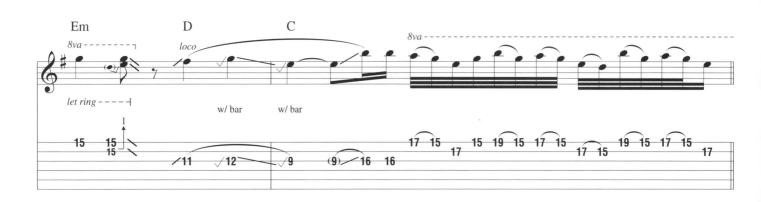

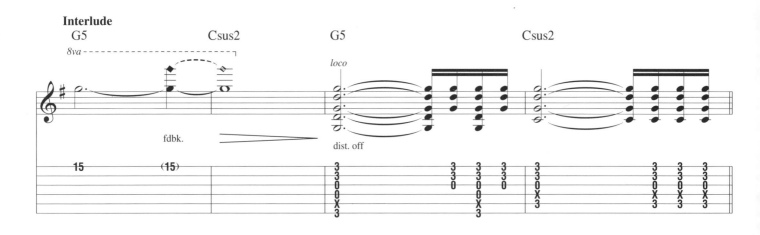

Interlude

Verse

3. I know I could-a saved a love that night _ if I'd known what to say. _

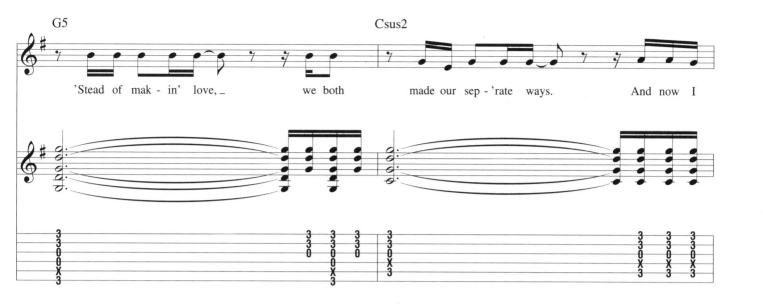

'Stead of mak-in' love, __ we both made our sep-'rate ways. And now I

hear you found some-bod-y new __ and that I nev-er meant that much to you. _____ To

hear that tears me up __ in - side, __ and to see you cuts me like a knife. __ I guess

Chorus

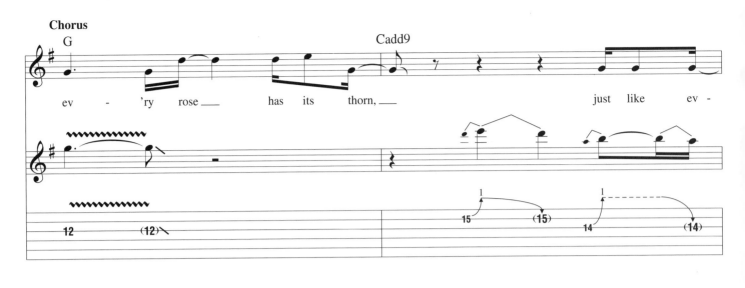

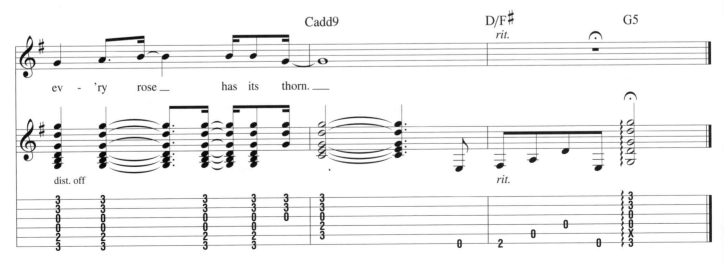

Fly to the Angels

Words and Music by Mark Slaughter and Dana Strum

Tune down 1 step:
(low to high) D-G-C-F-A-D

Intro

Moderate Rock ♩ = 120

Verse

1. Pic - tures of you, _____ oh, they're still on my ____ mind. ___
2. *See additional lyrics*

You had the smile _____ that could light ___ up ___ the world. ___

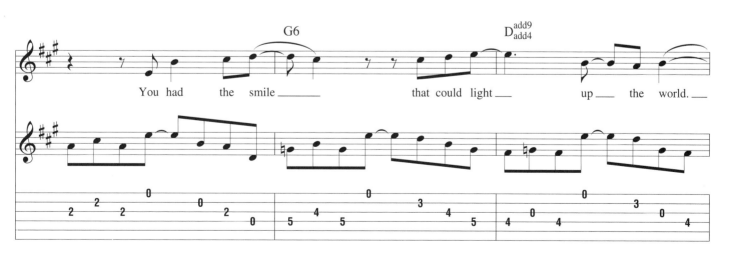

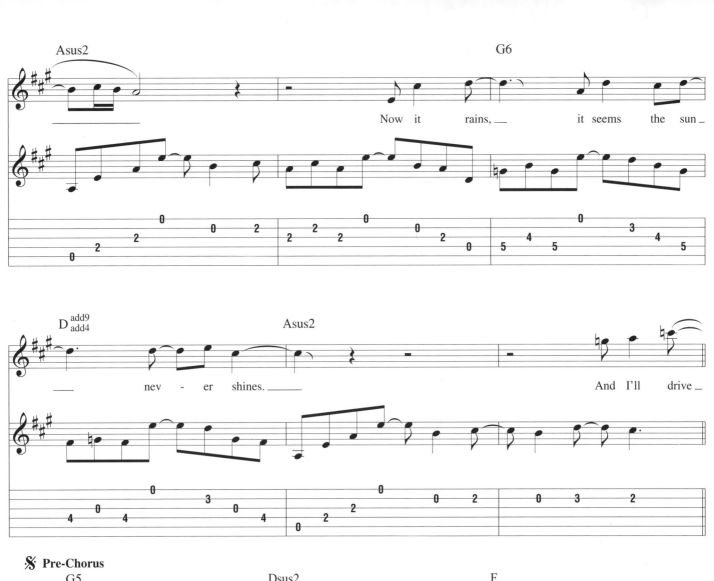

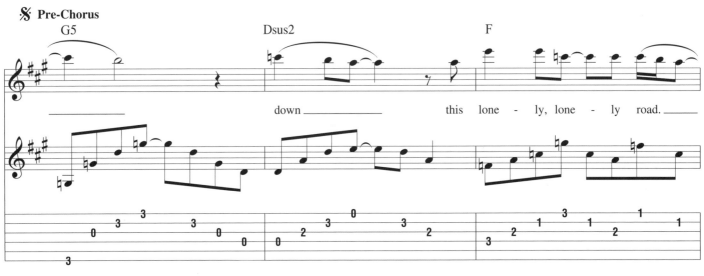

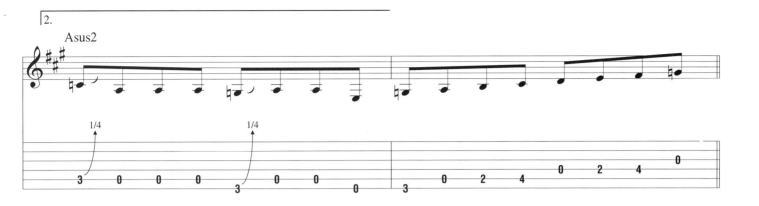

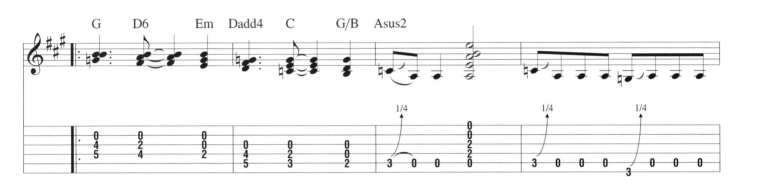

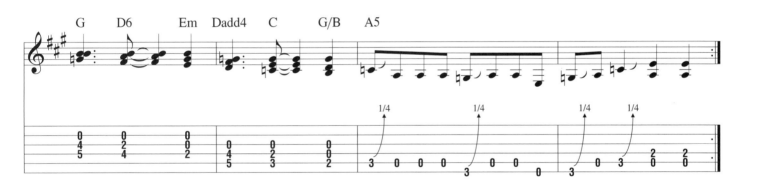

And still I drive _

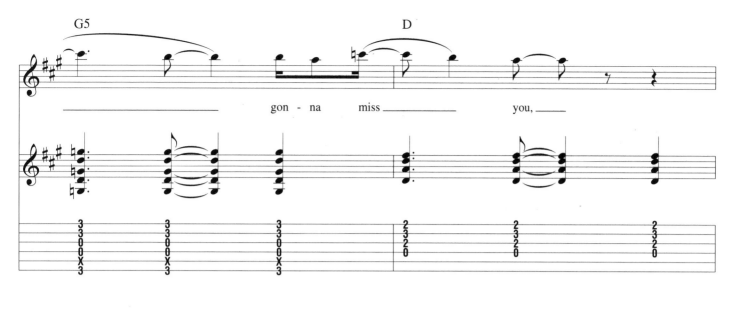

gon - na miss _____ you, _____

miss you, girl.

w/ clean tone

Free time
Asus2

Additional Lyrics

2. You know it hurts me way deep inside
   When I turn and look and find that you're not there.
   I try to convince myself that the pain,
   The pain, it's still not gone.

Hole Hearted

Words and Music by Nuno Bettencourt and Gary Cherone

Tune down 1/2 step:
(low to high) Eb-Ab-Db-Gb-Bb-Eb

Intro

Moderate Rock ♩ = 104

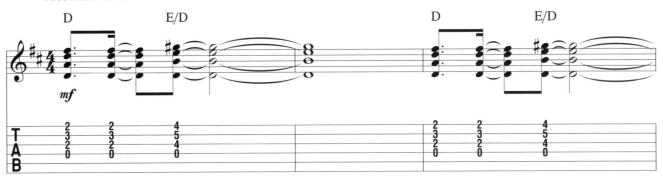

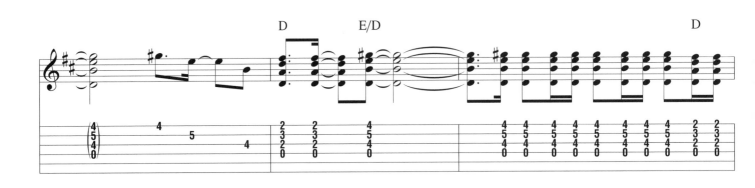

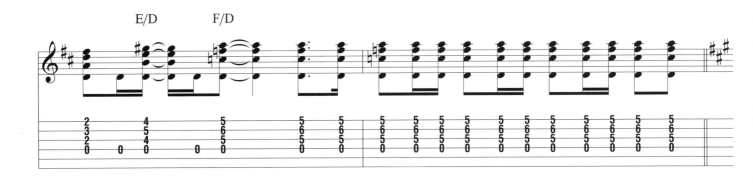

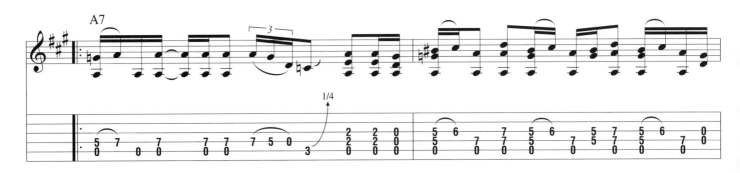

§ **Verse**

1. Life's am - bi - tions oc - cu - py my time.
2. *See additional lyrics*

Pri -

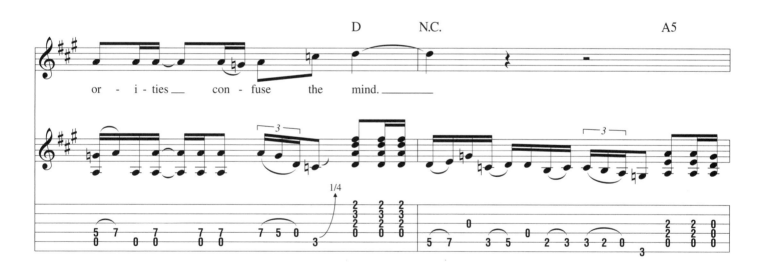

or - i - ties — con - fuse the mind. _____

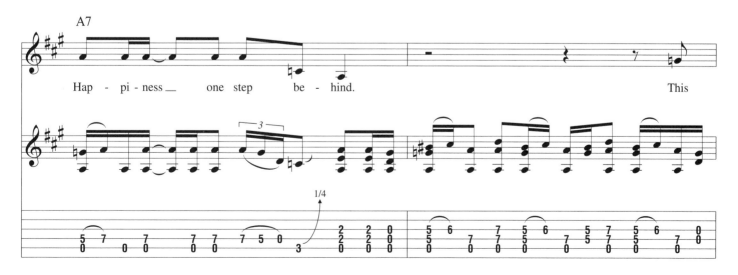

Hap - pi - ness — one step be - hind.

This

cir - cle ___ can't fit ___ where a square should _ be? ___ There's a

Chorus

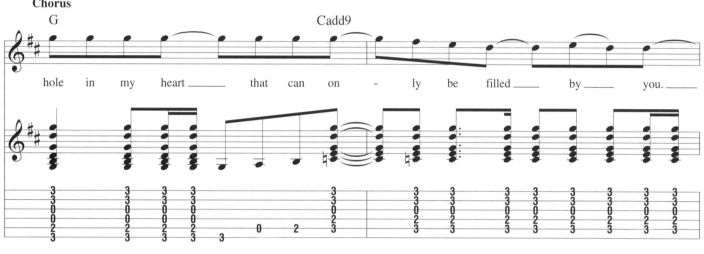

hole in my heart ___ that can on - ly be filled ___ by ___ you. ___

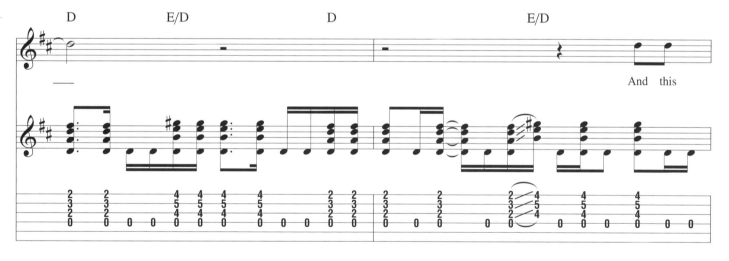

And this

To Coda ⊕

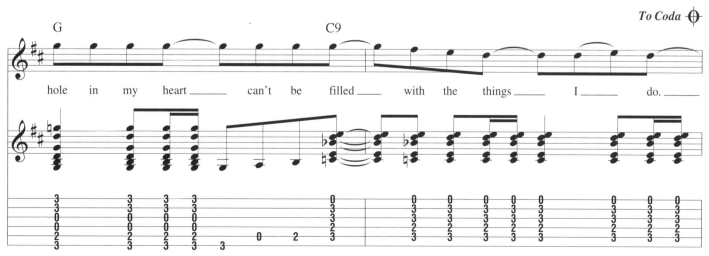

hole in my heart ___ can't be filled ___ with the things ___ I ___ do. ___

Hole heart - ed,

hole heart - ed.

Interlude

D.S. al Coda

2. This

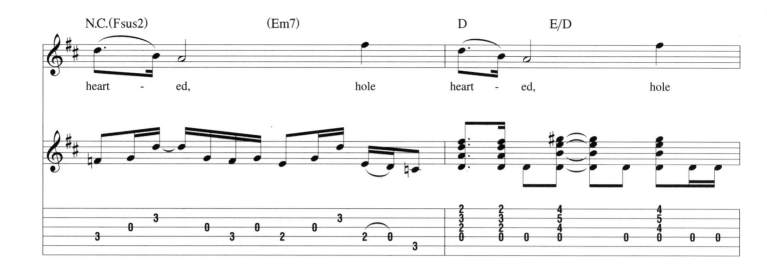

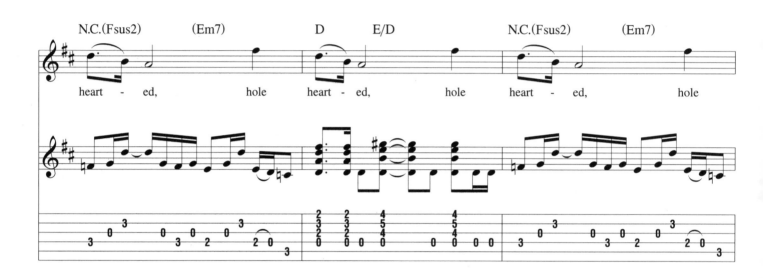

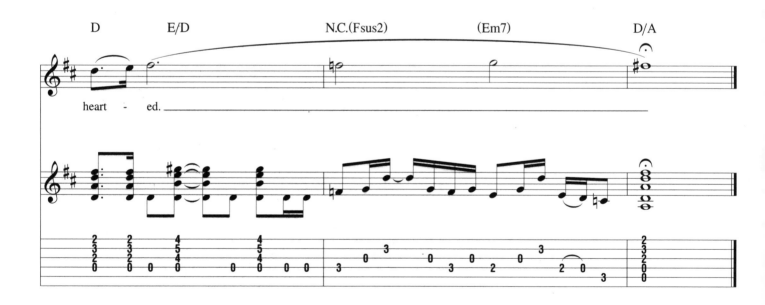

Additional Lyrics

2. This heart of stone is where I hide.
   These feet of clay kept warm inside.
   Day by day, less satisfied.
   Not fade away before I die.

Love of a Lifetime

Words and Music by Bill Leverty and Carl Snare

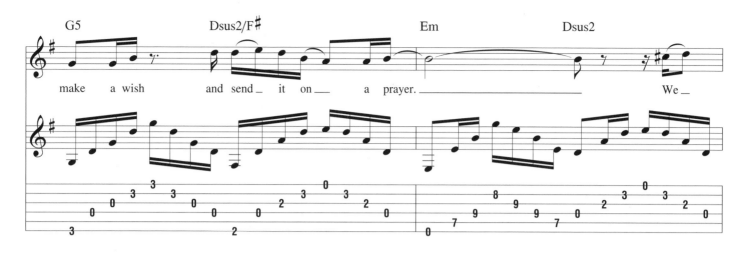

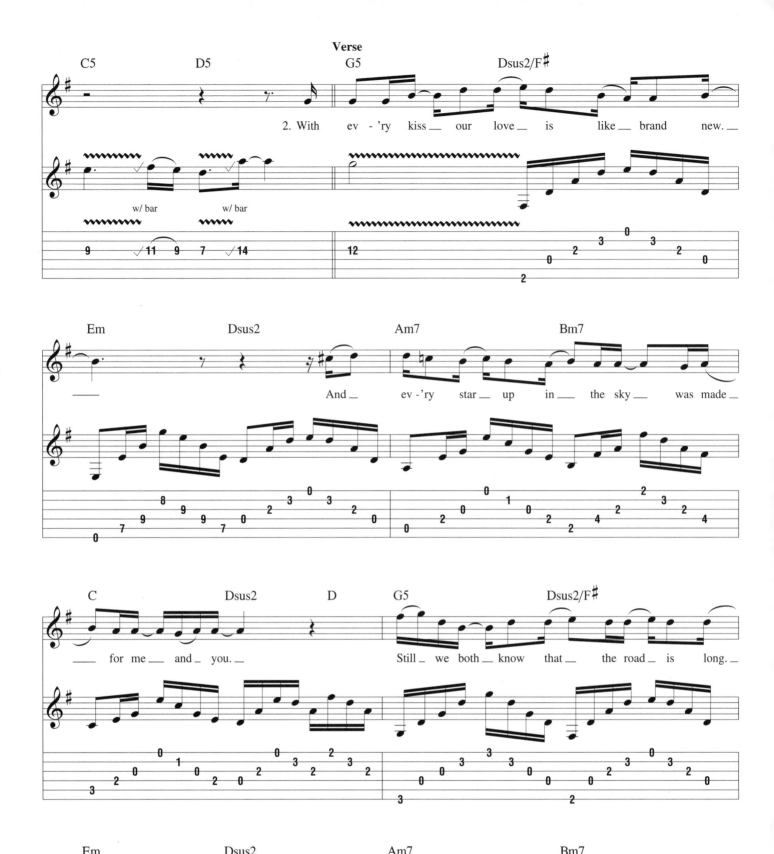

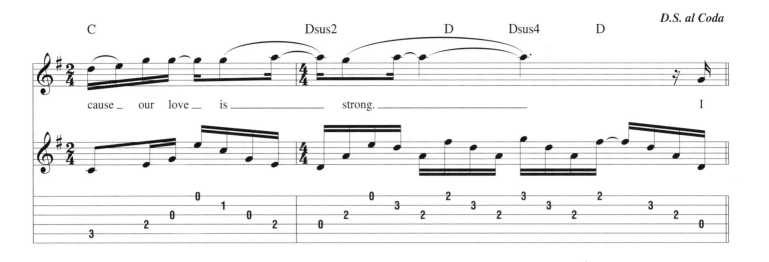

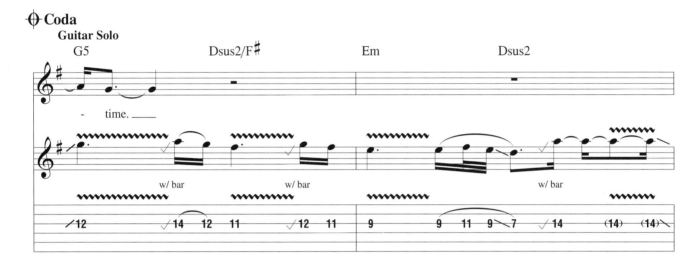

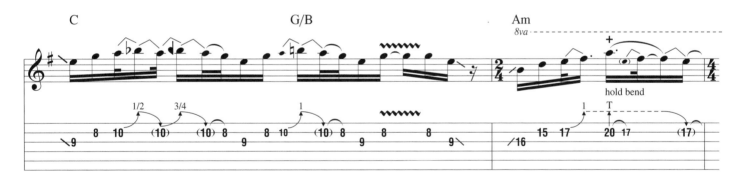

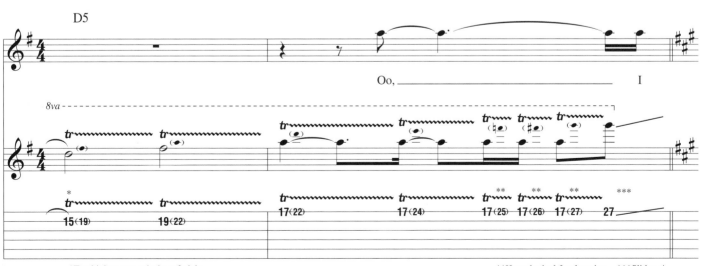

*Tap higher note w/ edge of pick.

**Hypothetical fret location.   ***Slide w/
edge of pick.

Chorus

Love Is on the Way

Words and Music by Jason Bieler

Let's stop the hands — of time. _____

Guitar Solo

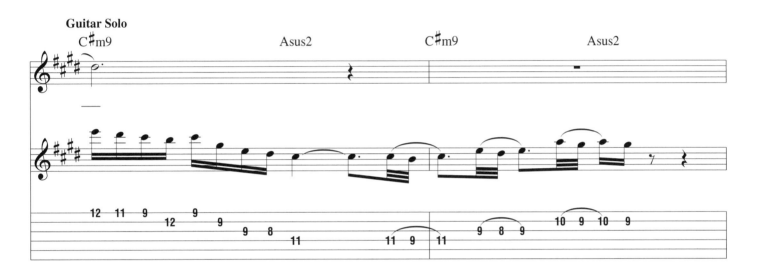

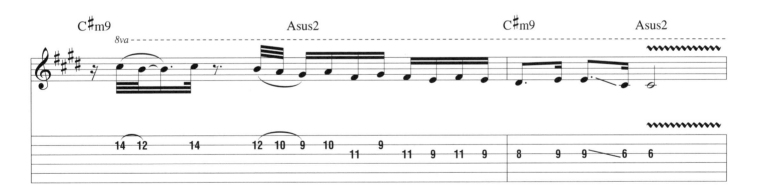

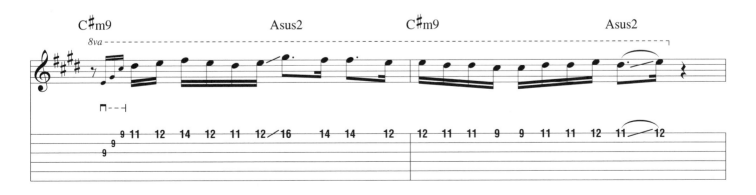

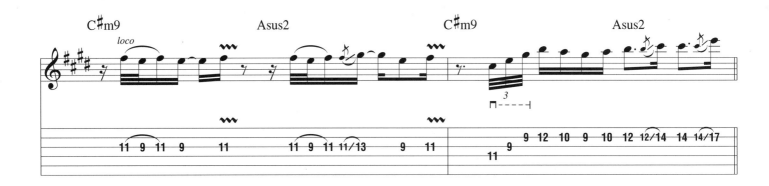

Outro-Chorus

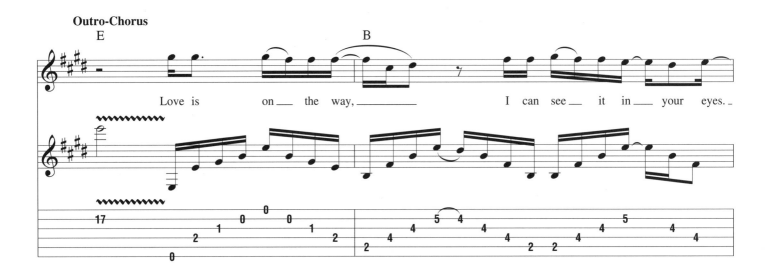

Love is on the way, _____ I can see ___ it in ___ your eyes. _

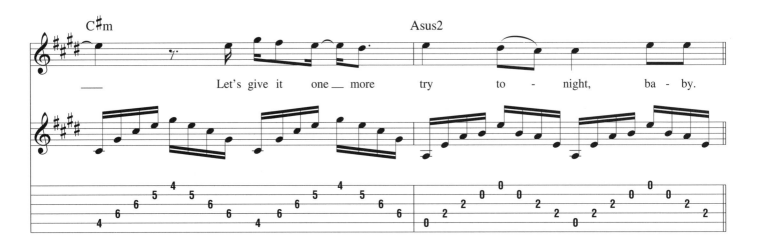

___ Let's give it one ___ more try to - night, ba - by.

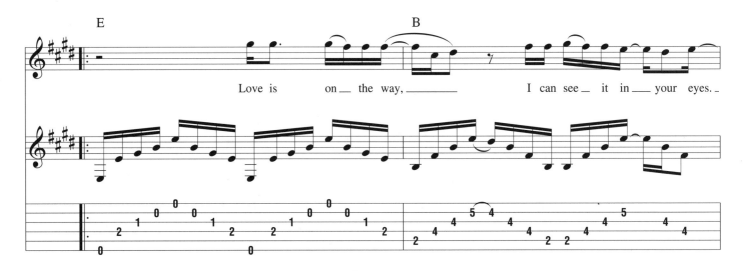

Love is on ___ the way, _____ I can see ___ it in ___ your eyes. _

Love is on ___ the way, _____ I can see ___ it in ___ your eyes. _

Love is on ___ the way, _____

Love is on ___ the way, _____ I can see ___ it in ___ your eyes. _

Love is on ___ the way, _____ I can see ___ it in ___ your eyes. _

Let's give it one — more try to - night, ba - by.

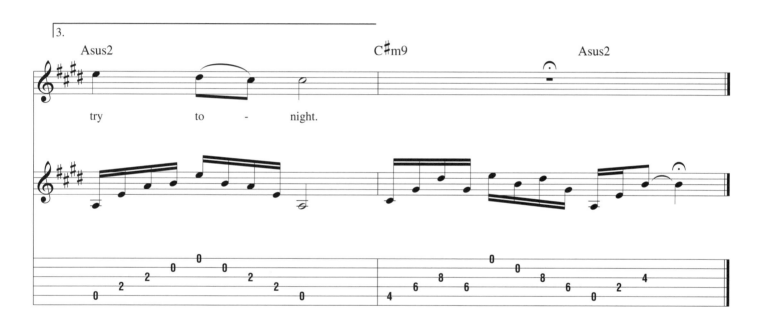

try to - night.

Additional Lyrics

2. Time of season wipes the tears.
No rhyme or reason, no more fears.
All the dreaming is far behind.
You are here now, and everything's alright.

To Be With You

Words and Music by Eric Martin and David Grahame

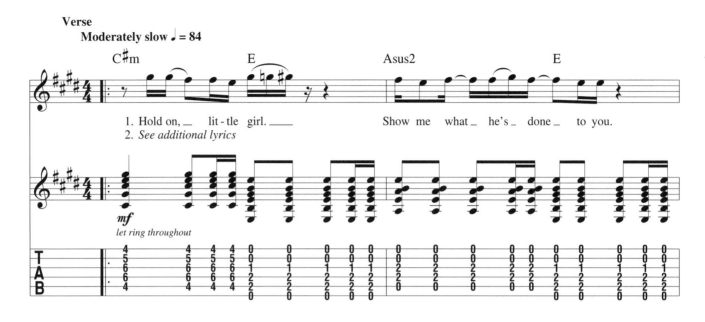

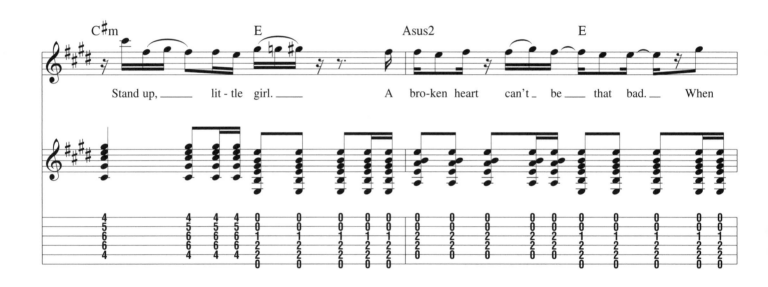

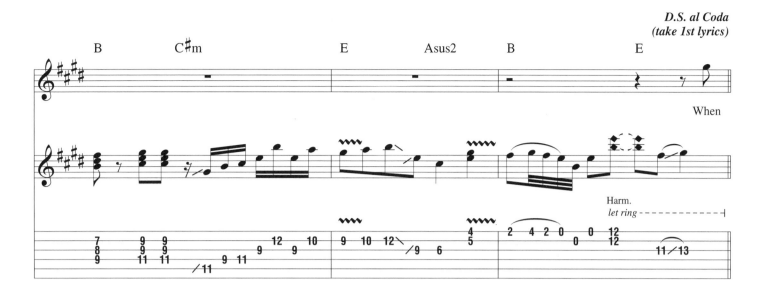

When

Harm.
let ring - - - - - - - - - - -|

Coda

Chorus
A tempo

Let me be ___ the one ___ to show ___ you.

(I'm the one who wants to

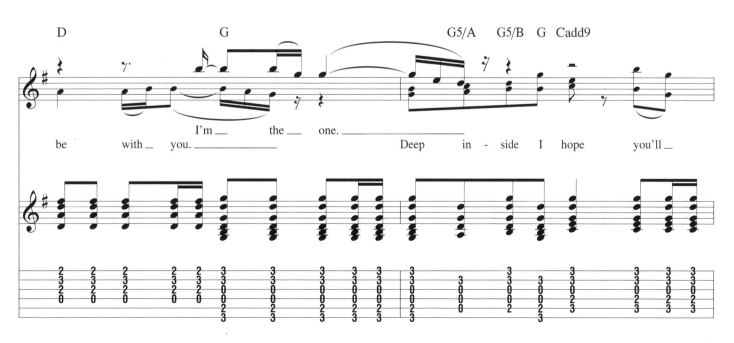

I'm ___ the ___ one. ___

Deep in - side I hope you'll ___

be with ___ you. ___

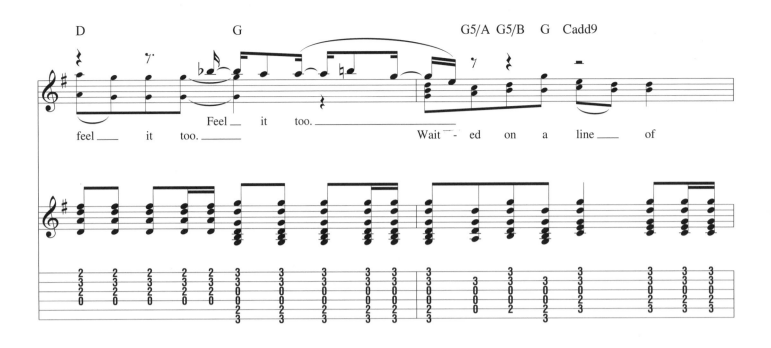

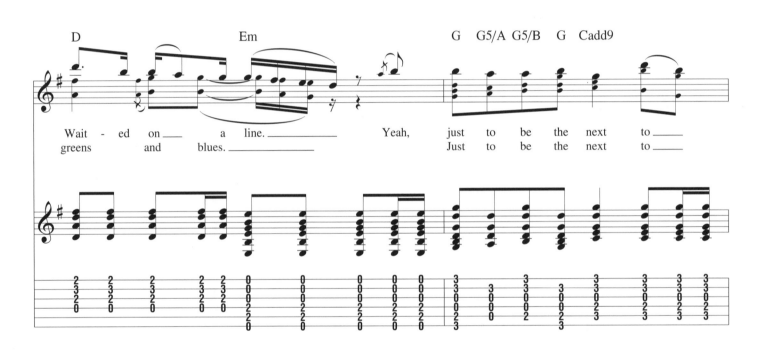

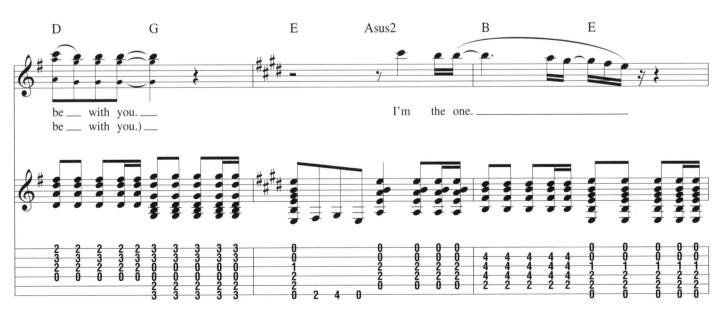

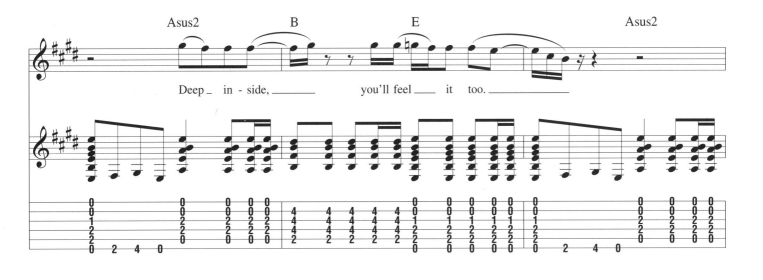

Deep _ in - side, _____ you'll feel ___ it too. ___

Wait-ed on _ that line. ___ Yeah, just to be the next to be ___ with you. ___

Outro

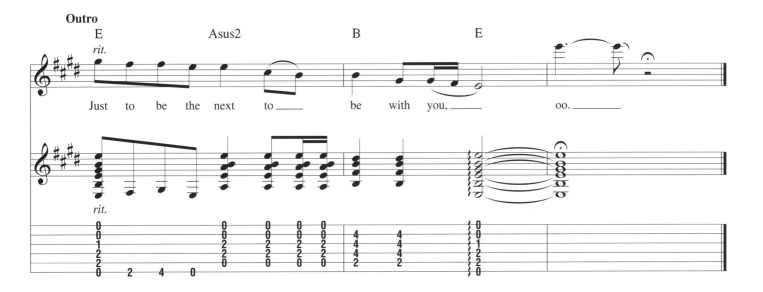

Just to be the next to _____ be with you, _____ oo. _____

Additional Lyrics

2. Build up your condfidence
   So you can be on top for once.
   Wake up. Who cares about
   Little boys that talk too much?
   I've seen it all go down.
   Your game of love was all rained out.
   So come on, baby, come on over.
   Let me be the one to hold you.

When the Children Cry

Words and Music by Mike Tramp and Vito Bratta

Intro
Moderately fast Ballad ♩ = 131

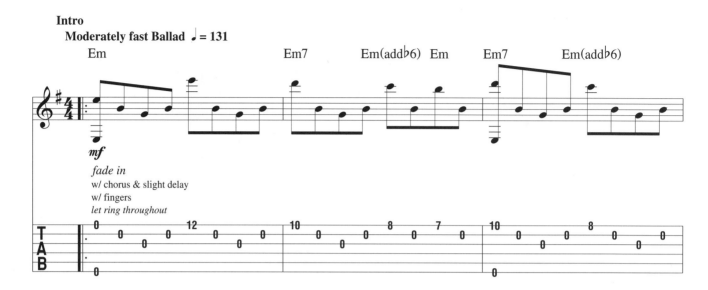

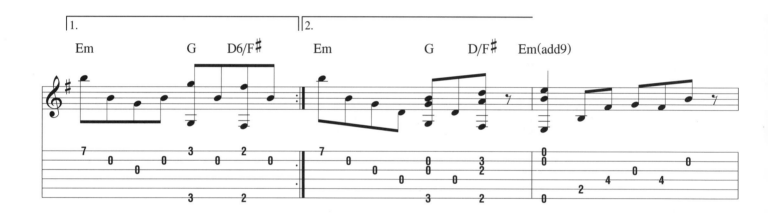

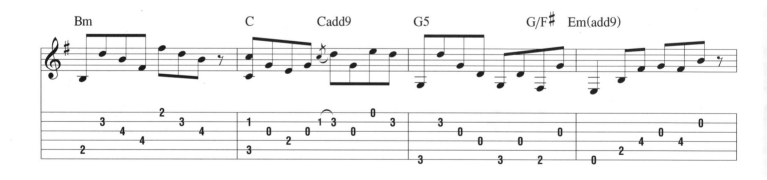

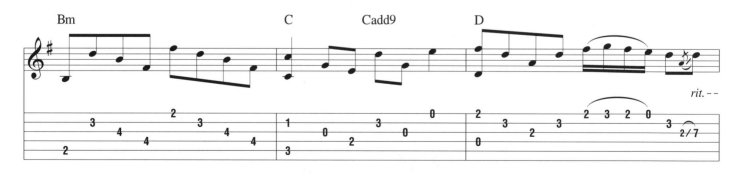

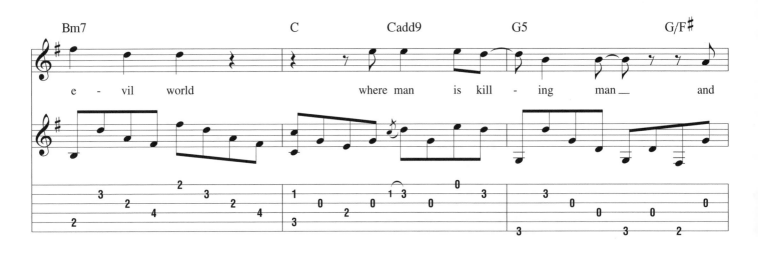

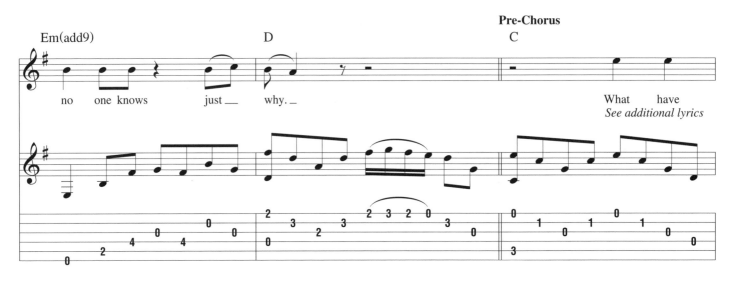

Pre-Chorus

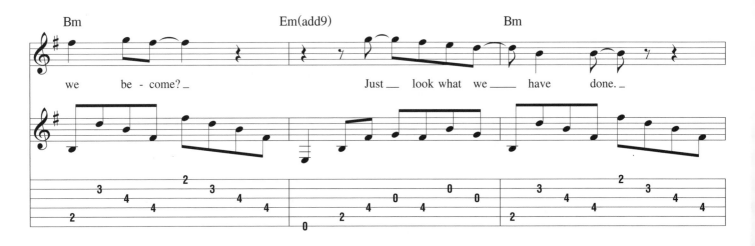

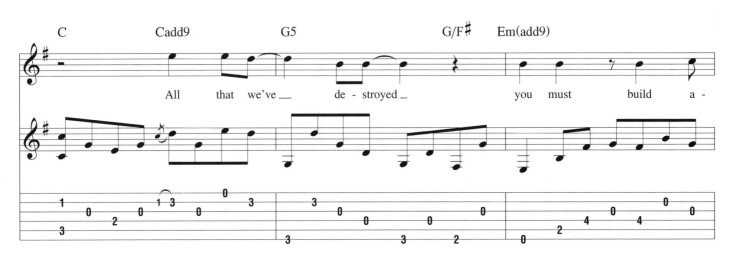

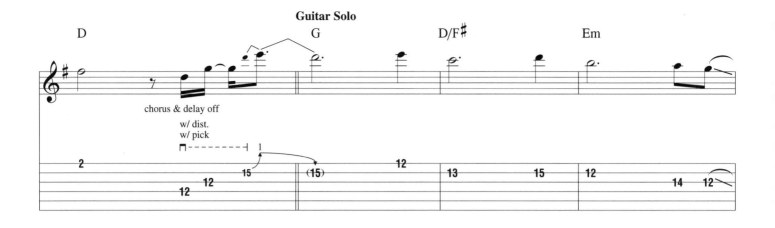

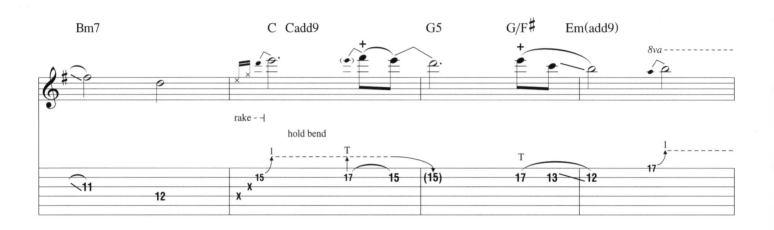

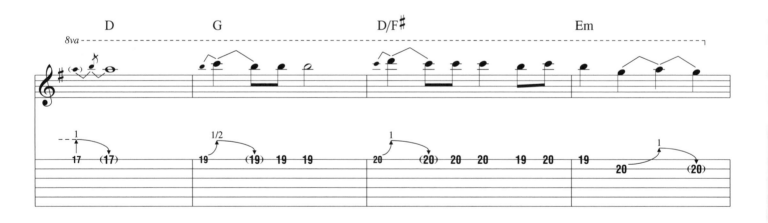

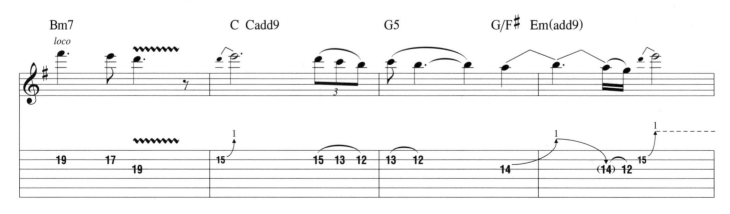

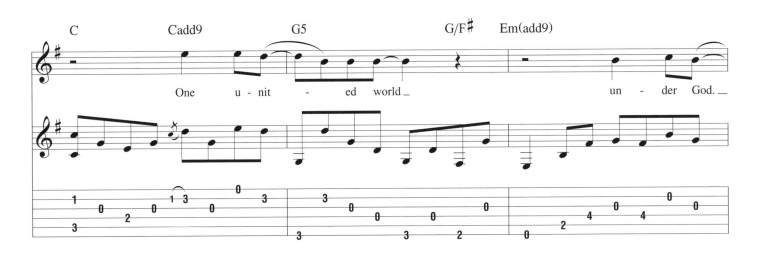

One u - nit - ed world _ un - der God. _

Outro-Chorus

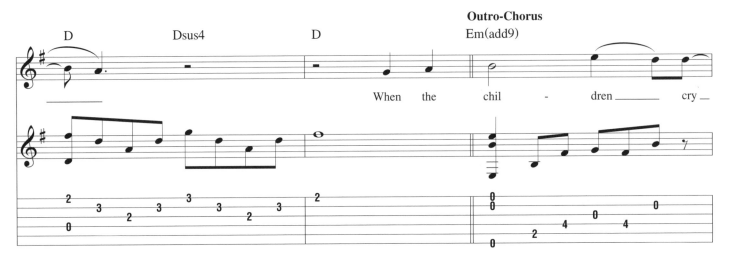

When the chil - dren _____ cry _

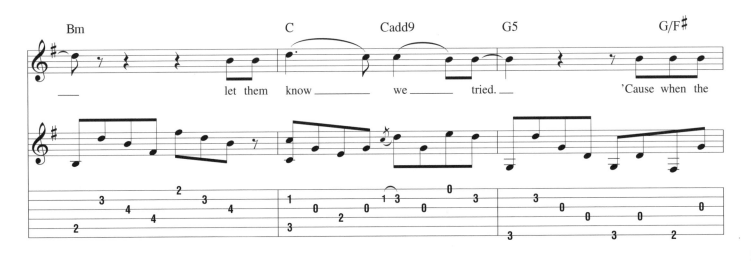

_ let them know _____ we _____ tried. _ 'Cause when the

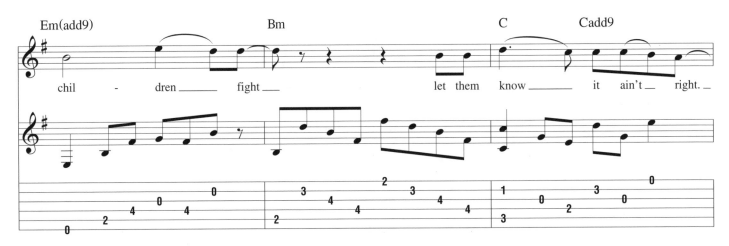

chil - dren _____ fight _ let them know _____ it ain't _ right. _

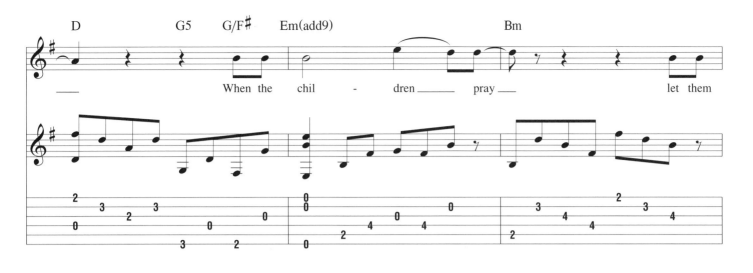

Additional Lyrics

2. Little child, you must show the way
   To a better day for all the young.
   'Cause you were born for all the world to see
   That we all can live with love and peace.

Pre-Chorus No more presidents.
   And all the wars will end.
   One united world under God.

Signs

Words and Music by Les Emmerson

Intro
Moderately slow ♩ = 82

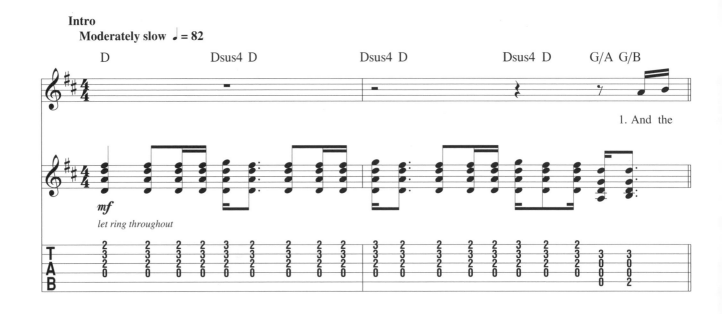

1. And the

Verse

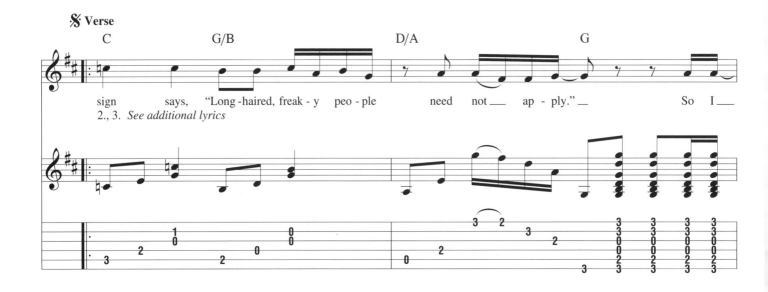

sign says, "Long-haired, freak-y peo-ple need not __ ap-ply." __ So I __
2., 3. *See additional lyrics*

__ tucked my hair up un-der my hat and I went in to ask him why. __

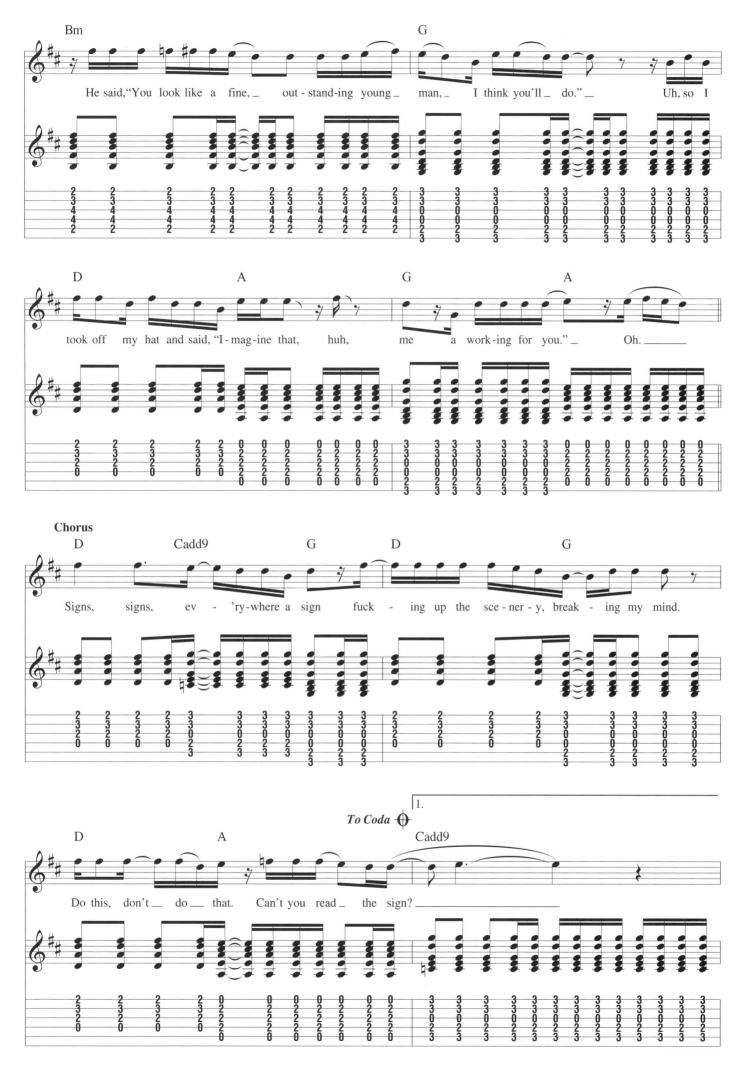

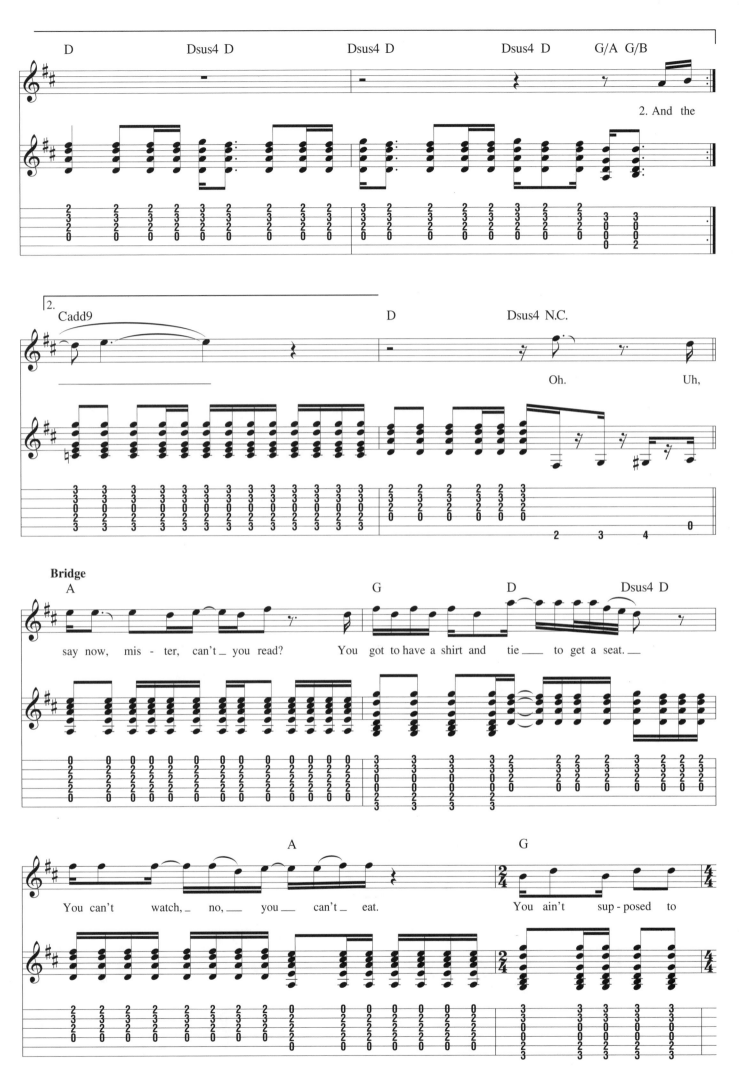

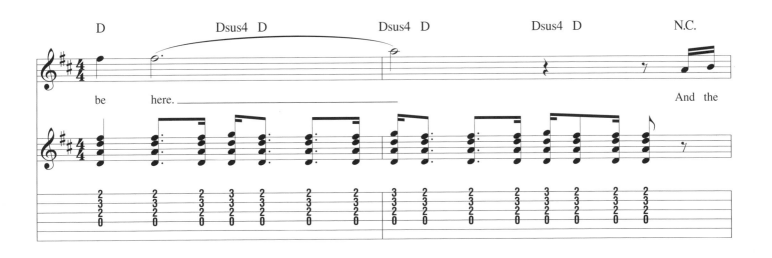

be here. _____ And the

sign said, "You got to have a mem-ber-ship card to get in - side." _ Ooh!

Guitar Solo

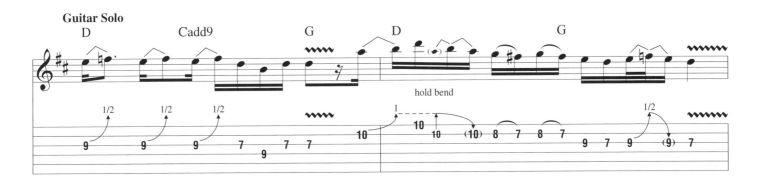

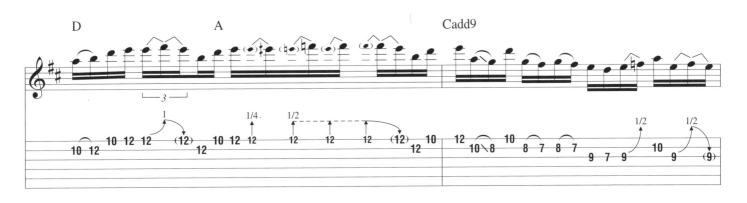

D.S. al Coda

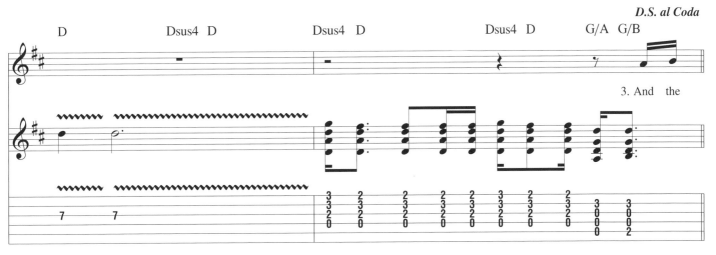

3. And the

Coda

Outro

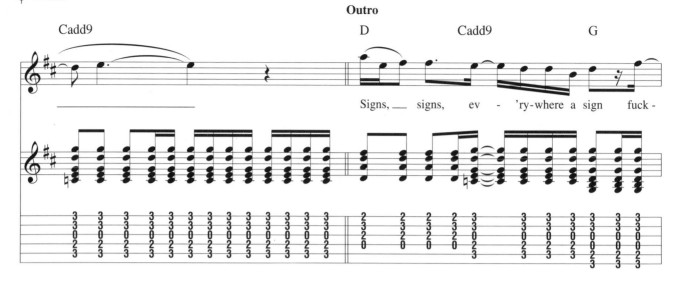

Signs, __ signs, ev - 'ry-where a sign fuck-

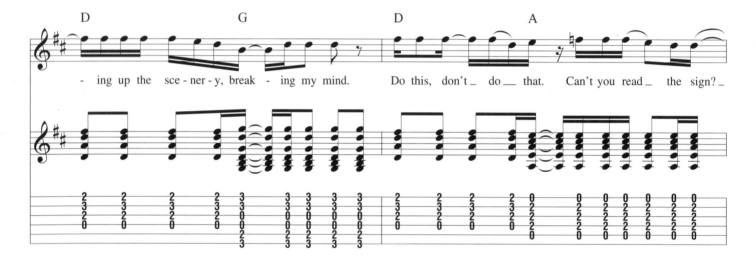

- ing up the sce - ner - y, break - ing my mind.   Do this, don't __ do __ that.   Can't you read __ the sign? __

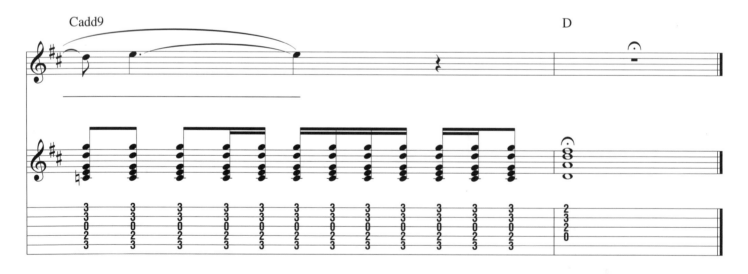

Additional Lyrics

2. And the sign says, "Anybody caught trespassing will be shot on sight."
   So I jumped the fence and yelled at the house, "Hey, what gives you the right
   To put up a fence to keep me out or to keep Mother Nature in?"
   If God was here he'd tell it to your face, "Man, you're some kinda sinner."

3. And the sign says, "Everybody welcome, come in and kneel down and pray."
   And then they pass around the plate at the end of it all, and I didn't have a penny to pay.
   So I got me a pen and paper, and I made up my own fuckin' sign.
   I said, "Thank you, Lord, for thinkin' about me, I'm alive and doing fine."